Cotswold] tl.. Northern Cotswolds

Designed
Written & Illustrated

by
Peter T. Reardon

Published by
REARDON PUBLISHING
PO Box 919, Cheltenham, Glos, GL50 9AN.
Website: www.Reardon.Biz
Email: nicholasreardon@aol.com
tel: 01242 231800

Copyright © 1976
Reardon Publishing

20th Edition 2017

Designed, Written and Illustrated
by
Peter T Reardon

ISBN 9781873877883

Printed
in the
Cotswold Area

THE COTSWOLDS

The Cotswolds, with their beauty supreme,
A rambler's pleasure, an artist's dream.
Within these undulating hills abound
Enjoyment for all, in sight and sound.

Tall trees give a proud and noble scene,
Whilst the fields show a calm and placid green.
The dawns and sunsets give colourful thrills
When viewed from the tops of these glorious hills.

Ancient buildings and monuments are to be found
In towns whose names have a very quaint sound,
And streams and rivers wend their musical way
Past banks, with wild flowers, both colourful and gay.

In winter, the hills appear harsh and foreboding
In their white coats of snow and caps of grey clouding,
From the strong, icy winds, there is little respite
Howling and whistling by day and by night.

Cotswold beauty survives winter without coming to harm
And returns in the new spring with added charm.

ALFRED KING

INTRODUCTION

The Cotswolds

The beauty of the Cotswolds is not new. It is not something that has just come about recently. It is, you might even say, as old as the hills themselves. To the visitor from other parts, it has a unique splendour all it's own. To those fortunate enough to live here, it is seen in a different way. Through the ages this beauty has been captured by the artist's brush, the pen of the writer and in more recent times, the camera lens of the photographer. There are many fine paintings in existence of the great country houses in wonderful settings, and much has been written of the towns and villages of the Cotswolds. But it is not only beauty to be found in these hills, they are rich in history also.

Some 4,000 years ago, man thought the Cotswolds the ideal place in which to live, as can be seen from the number of camp sites and long barrows that can be found. From those days, right through to more recent times with the famous Red Arrows Aerobatic Team based at Kemble, near Cirencester, and test flights of Concorde from Fairford, the Cotswolds have been significant in the history of this country. In this little book it is hoped to acquaint you, in pictures with some of the details that have gone to make up this wonderful history.

With that, it could mean a better appreciation of, and happier memories of a more enjoyable visit to the Cotswolds.

PETER T. REARDON

Bibury

Bibury must surely be one of the most unchanged villages in the Cotswolds though one of the most frequently visited. The church, acquired by the Monks of Osney, was partly rebuilt on the site of an earlier building. A number of architectural periods in the fabric are of some interest, as are the cast of an Anglo-Saxon tombstone dated around 1000 AD, the original being held in the British Museum. Tombstones in the floor of the nave go back to 1700 and a brass plaque on the chancel arch is to the memory of Frederick George, 5th Baron of Sherborne and Vicar of the parish for 42 years. On the outside a good Norman doorway can be seen in the north wall, also a stone, believed to be a tombstone of early Saxon times built into the north wall of the Chancel. This little feature is shown in the drawing on the right.

Bisley

A village lying about 3 miles east of Stroud and has many features to offer the visitor to the Cotswolds. The little sketch below shows part of the Seven Springs of Bisley. The water comes from natural springs and has not been known to dry up. Each year, a ceremony called Well Dressing takes place on Ascension Day when the children dress up for this special occasion. Its origins probably go back to pagan worship. In those days it was believed that to pacify the water spirits ensured a constant flow from the springs, this being very important to the local people of the day as there was no piped water to supplement it. The church has many interesting relics for the visitor to browse over, some going back as far as Roman times. The churchyard is not without its interest too, maybe foremost being a monument, hexagonal and with a spire surmounted by a cross. The structure is supposed to cover an ancient well, the legend being, that after a local priest had fallen into it and drowned, the well was sealed up.

LOWER SLAUGHTER - GLOS.

Bourton on the Water

Much favoured by tourists from all over the world, Bourton on the Water has quite a variety of interests to offer. The Model Village is a must when visiting Bourton, and can be seen in the grounds of the Old New Inn. It is of course, a model of Bourton on the Water. Birdland, with a diversity of species in all their magnificence of colour is an attraction which thrills young and old alike, and one that should not be missed. Art galleries form part of the scene of Bourton with their air of sobriety, paralleled only by that of the museums. At the Perfumery, it is possible to sample some of the wonderful perfumes actually made and blended on the premises. The Motor Museum really is different. An interesting assemblage of some old favourites, also Britains largest collection of signs associated with motoring. Afternoon teas with homemade cakes are to be enjoyed at several pleasing tea-rooms offering their services. The sketch above shows two little stone figures to be found flanking the entrance to the Model Village. The drawing below shows the skull and crossbones over the west door of the Church of St. Lawrence. Bourton is on the famous Fosse Way, or A429 as we know it today. Just a few miles from Bourton on the Water is the village of Lower Slaughter (pictured opposite). The large sketch shows the river Windrush and the Lower Slaughter Mill, which is also the bakery for this part of the Cotswolds. Here one can see a village which is still unspoilt by the relentless tread of the 20th century.

Lower Slaughter is easy to find being just off the Fosse Way between Bourton and Stow on the Wold.

Broadway Tower

The picture below shows a large tower standing on a spot known as Broadway Beacon, right on the edge of the Cotswold escarpment. It was built by the Earl of Coventry for his Countess, who wondered if a fire built on this spot could be seen from their family home at Croome Court. It could be, so the tower was built. During the summer months the tower is open to the public and from the top the views on a clear day are breathtaking. It is possible to see into as many as twelve counties and must surely be one of the finest viewpoints in this part of the country. Broadway Tower is reached by turning south off the A44 Broadway to Moreton in Marsh road at the top of Fish Hill, which overlooks Broadway. The lane adjacent to the tower follows part of Buckle Street, one of the old Roman Roads.

Burford

Although in Oxfordshire, Burford is popularly known as "The Gateway to the Cotswolds". There is much here to interest the visitor to this town with it's historic buildings and, pictured here, the Tolsey, now a museum. At the north end of town is a fine example of a packhorse bridge while in the High Street are many good Inns and coaching houses. The town has very early associations with transport and travel and, lying on the River Windrush as it does the name was possibly derived from burn, meaning stream and ford, meaning crossing. Burford is situated on the north side of the junction of the A40 Cheltenham to Oxford and London road with the A361 Chipping Norton to Swindon road.

Cainscross

In the year of 1894 a decision was made to amalgamate the neighbouring parishes with that of Cainscross into a single parish of that name. Lying in the Frome Valley between Stroud and Stonehouse it is in the centre of the cloth manufacturing industry. The little picture on the right shows an unusual mile stone which possibly stood at the centre of the old parish of Cainscross, now still taking its place at a roundabout in the centre of modern Cainscross. On the plate just visible on the left of the shaft it claims 'To Stroud 1 Mile'. On the south and east sides of the lantern type head are sundials, while on the remaining sides are the inscriptions 'Behold now is the accepted time' and 'Seek ye the Lord while He may be found'. Grave thoughts perhaps, considering its present position on a busy road junction, but was quite suitable when just erected and the people of the valley had time to stop and think on these things. Cainscross straddles the A419 and is easily accessible from Stroud on the A46 or the A38 and Motorway, junction 13 to Stroud.

Chipping Campden

Famous the world over, Chipping Campden boasts architectural gems in the Cotswold style unchanged for hundreds of years. The Market Hall, of which a view through an archway is shown here, was built in the 17th century by Sir Baptist Hicks. Although a London merchant, Sir Baptist chose to live at Chipping Campden and had a beautiful mansion built close to the church. It was, unfortunately, mostly destroyed during the Civil War and only a handful of remains exist today. The gateway still stands though not complete. Sir Baptist Hicks was also responsible for the building of the Almshouses near the church, perhaps the most popular place in Campden for artists and photographers. Sir William Grevel, wool merchant and benefactor of the town, leaves his home as a memorial to those days of wealth.

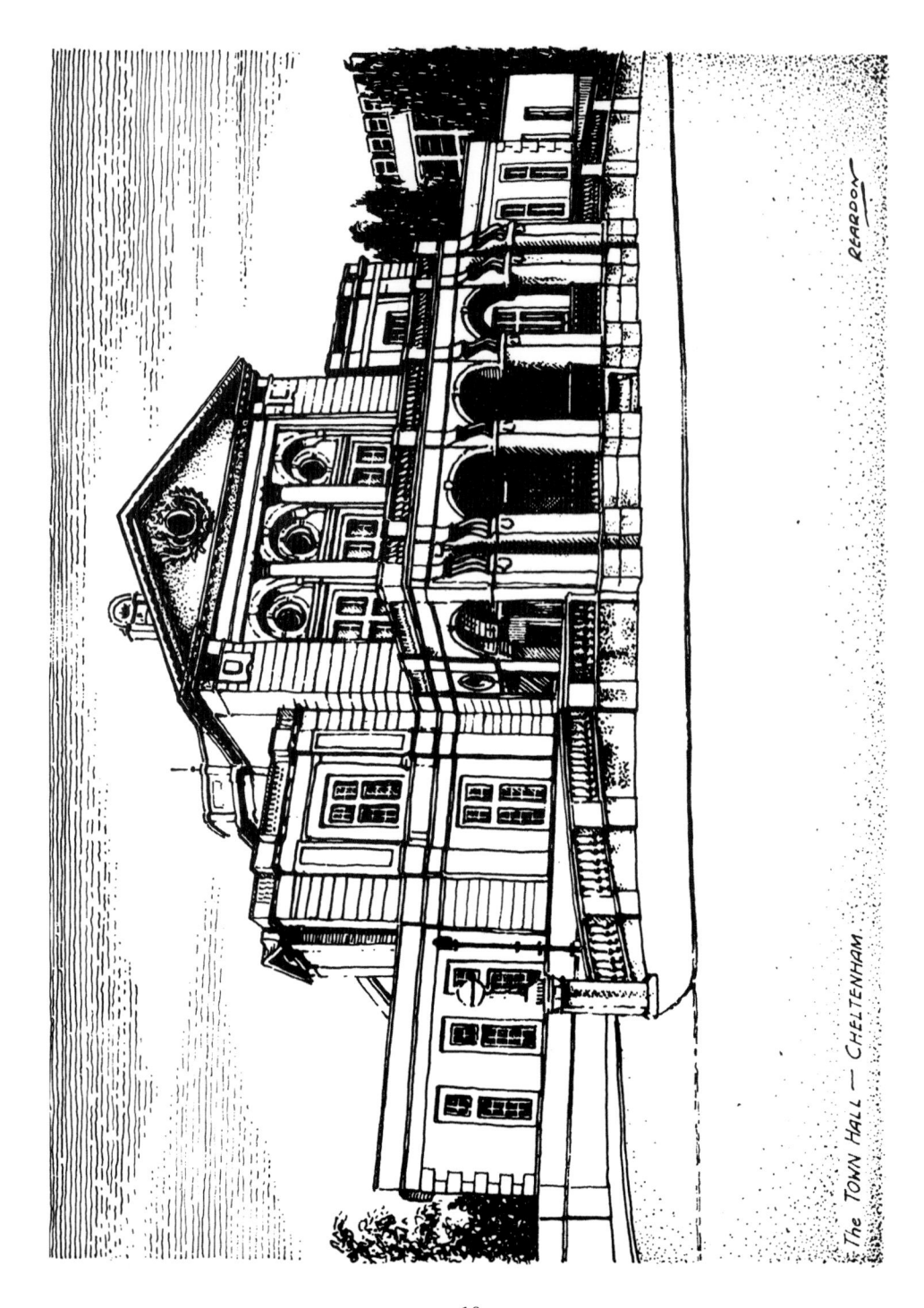

The Town Hall — Cheltenham

Cheltenham

Cheltenham Spa situated under the Cotswold escarpment is an ideal place to base oneself when touring the Cotswolds. In fact, it is such a lovely Regency town it is itself a major Cotswold attraction. The main picture to the left is that of Cheltenham Town Hall, just off the Promenade in Imperial Square. The Town Hall is an impressive building which has been the venue for a whole range of events from Flower Shows and Dances to Literary Festivals and Conferences. The decorative lamp, small sketch to the right, is one of two, mounted like sentinels on stone pillars at the foot of the steps leading up into the Minicipal Offices in Cheltenham's Tree lined Promenade.

St. Mary's Church, Cheltenham

Cheltenham is noted for its fine public buildings, shops, colleges and by no means least its churches. Pictured here on the right is the magnificent 15ft. Rose window to be found in the north transcept of the famous Parish Church of St. Mary, right in the centre of Cheltenham. The church spire is visible from several points in the town but because it is surrounded by tall shops and buildings, the church cannot be seen from the road. Due to this seclusion an air of tranquility reigns making it a place to pause for a moment and collect oneself. Inside the church, the impression of space and grandeur somewhat belies the external appearance. The colour in the finely-traceried windows and the exquisite carving of a screen in the south transcept and chancel add to the wonder of this place of worship. The walls are rich in tablets and brasses of celebrated people who have lived and died in and around Cheltenham.

Cirencester

A town with something to suit most tastes, Cirencester has a long and interesting history. Better known perhaps for its connections with the Roman period, it is not lacking in more recent historical evidence. The town grew under Roman rule as an administration centre, being situated at the junction of Ermine Street, the Fosse Way and Akeman Street. Being second only in size and importance to London, it was fortified against attack and a section of the east wall and bastion as it is today just north of the Fosse Way is shown in the sketch above. There is an excellent museum of Roman remains in Park Street, a testimonial to the high standard of work and living of those times. Many of the roads today follow the routes of the old Roman Imperial Posting Roads like part of the A417, the A429 Cirencester to Halford, 12 miles north of Moreton-in-Marsh, passing Northleach and nudging Bourton-on-the-Water and Stow-on-the-Wold as it goes along. The route of the Fosse Way can be travelled by major and minor roads nearly all the way to its end at Lincoln. Construction of these great roads, which were built mainly for military purposes, was basically similar to the way ours are built today. First the direction of the road was sighted out by the Roman engineers, the construction gangs following in their wake digging out the foundations and either driving in heavy timbers end on or placing very large stones as a base. A layer of cemented big stones was followed by a layer of gravel or small stones mixed with cement and topped with large flat stones cemented in position. Edging stones were built up to contain the fabric of the road to the full depth. The drawing on the right is of a tablet indicating the position of the original edge-set stone on a part of the Fosse Way, now the A429. This tablet can be found about half way between Stow-on-the-Wold and Moreton-in-Marsh.

Compton Abdale, (The Crocodile)

In the Cotswolds, springs have always been looked upon with some reverence, possibly because at one time it was the only source of local water. These springs gush forth from odd places, each being individual in their own way; a muddy pool at Thames Head not far from Cirencester, recessed wall at Chalford, canopied outlet at Shipton Oliffe, ornate design for 7 springs at Bisley, plain large trough at Stow-on-the-Wold and, pictured here on the right, the bizarre, the head of a crocodile. This head can be found at the road junction in Compton Abdale just close to the church. Compton Abdale lies about 5 miles west of Northleach on the south side of the A40 Northleach to Oxford road. The crocodile head has been the object of many a motor club treasure hunt.

Didbrook

Nestling under the western escarpment of the Cotswolds lies the little village of Didbrook. A mile along a footpath to the south are the ruins of the once great Hailes Abbey. The Church, that of St. George, featured in the Wars of the Roses. In 1471, the Battle of Tewkesbury took place, but the widespread slaughter was not confined to around Tewkesbury. Apparently, a handful of Lancastrian soldiers sought refuge in the little church at Didbrook. This was, however, to no avail for they were discovered by the Yorkists, put against the oak door and shot. It is claimed that this is one of the first times that hand guns were used in this country. The Abbot of Hailes Abbey, who was also the Rector of St. George's at Didbrook, was so distressed at this desecration that he had the church torn down and rebuilt at his own expense. It is strange, but whether by design or for any other reason the church is unique in that there is neither a north or south door, just a single west door. Much material from the old building must have been used in the new one, since the bullet marks from that day are still in the old oak door.

—ON THE EDGE OF THE COTSWOLDS
THE 'LAMB INN' at FILKINS, in OXFORDSHIRE.—

Filkins

On the right is a sketch of another little lock-up, this time in the village of Filkins, just over the border in Oxfordshire. Not much room inside for one person, never mind two. The chains, and what looks like a massive bear trap would not be conducive to a restful night, especially during the summer. The opening in the door is only about six inches square so ventilation was limited, and only the spout of a pot could be got between the iron bars across the hole if the prisoner wanted a drink. On the opposite page is the Lamb Inn only a few short steps from the lock-up described above. It's possible that the reveller, starting in the Lamb, finished up in the Lock-up. Filkins, once the home of the late Sir Stafford Cripps and Lady Cripps, has benefitted much by their benevolence. They presented a Hall and Centre to the village, constructed by local craftsmen using local materials. After the death of Sir Stafford, Lady Cripps moved to Minchinhampton. Filkins can be found on the east side of the A361 about midway between Burford and Lechlade in Gloucestershire.

The Four Shires Stone

This large monumental looking structure can be found nearly 2 miles to the east of Moreton-in-Marsh on the A44 Chipping Norton road. It marks a spot where some years ago the boundaries of the four counties of Gloucestershire, Oxfordshire, Warwickshire and Worcestershire used to meet. In 1935 the county boundaries were adjusted and Worcestershire does not now meet here, the nearest point of this county boundary being about 5 miles due west of Moreton-in-Marsh at a place called Spring Hill House.

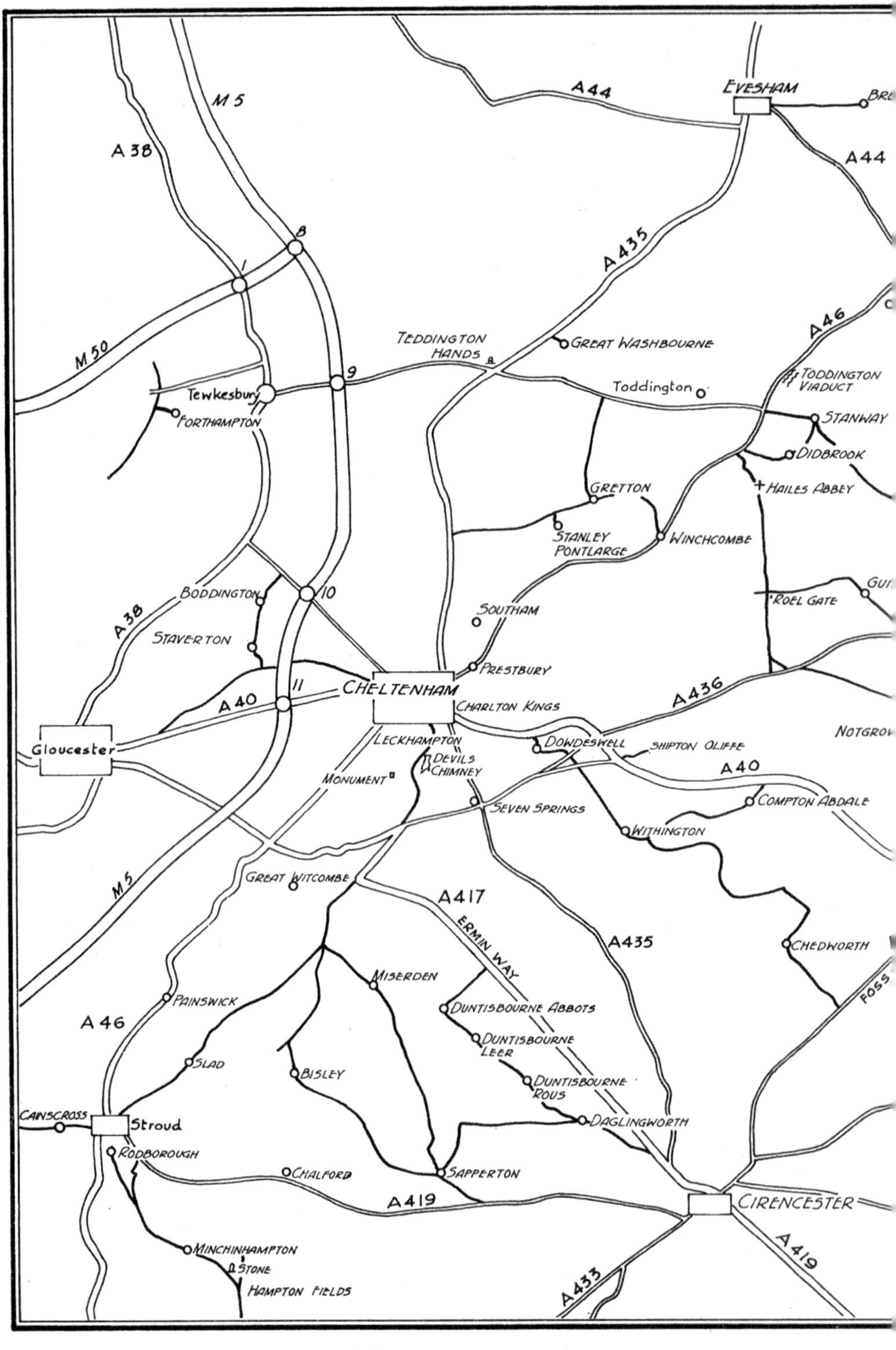
EVESHAM
A44
A44
M5
A38
8
1
M50
A435
A46
TEDDINGTON HANDS
GREAT WASHBOURNE
Tewkesbury
9
Toddington
TODDINGTON VIADUCT
STANWAY
FORTHAMPTON
DIDBROOK
HAILES ABBEY
GRETTON
STANLEY PONTLARGE
WINCHCOMBE
BODDINGTON
10
ROEL GATE
A38
SOUTHAM
STAVERTON
PRESTBURY
11
CHELTENHAM
A40
A436
CHARLTON KINGS
Gloucester
LECKHAMPTON
DOWDESWELL
SHIPTON OLIFFE
DEVILS CHIMNEY
A40
MONUMENT
SEVEN SPRINGS
COMPTON ABDALE
WITHINGTON
GREAT WITCOMBE
M5
A417
ERMIN WAY
A435
CHEDWORTH
MISERDEN
PAINSWICK
DUNTISBOURNE ABBOTS
A46
DUNTISBOURNE LEER
SLAD
BISLEY
DUNTISBOURNE ROUS
CAINSCROSS
Stroud
DAGLINGWORTH
RODBOROUGH
CHALFORD
SAPPERTON
A419
CIRENCESTER
A419
MINCHINHAMPTON
STONE
HAMPTON FIELDS
A433

Cotswold Driveabout

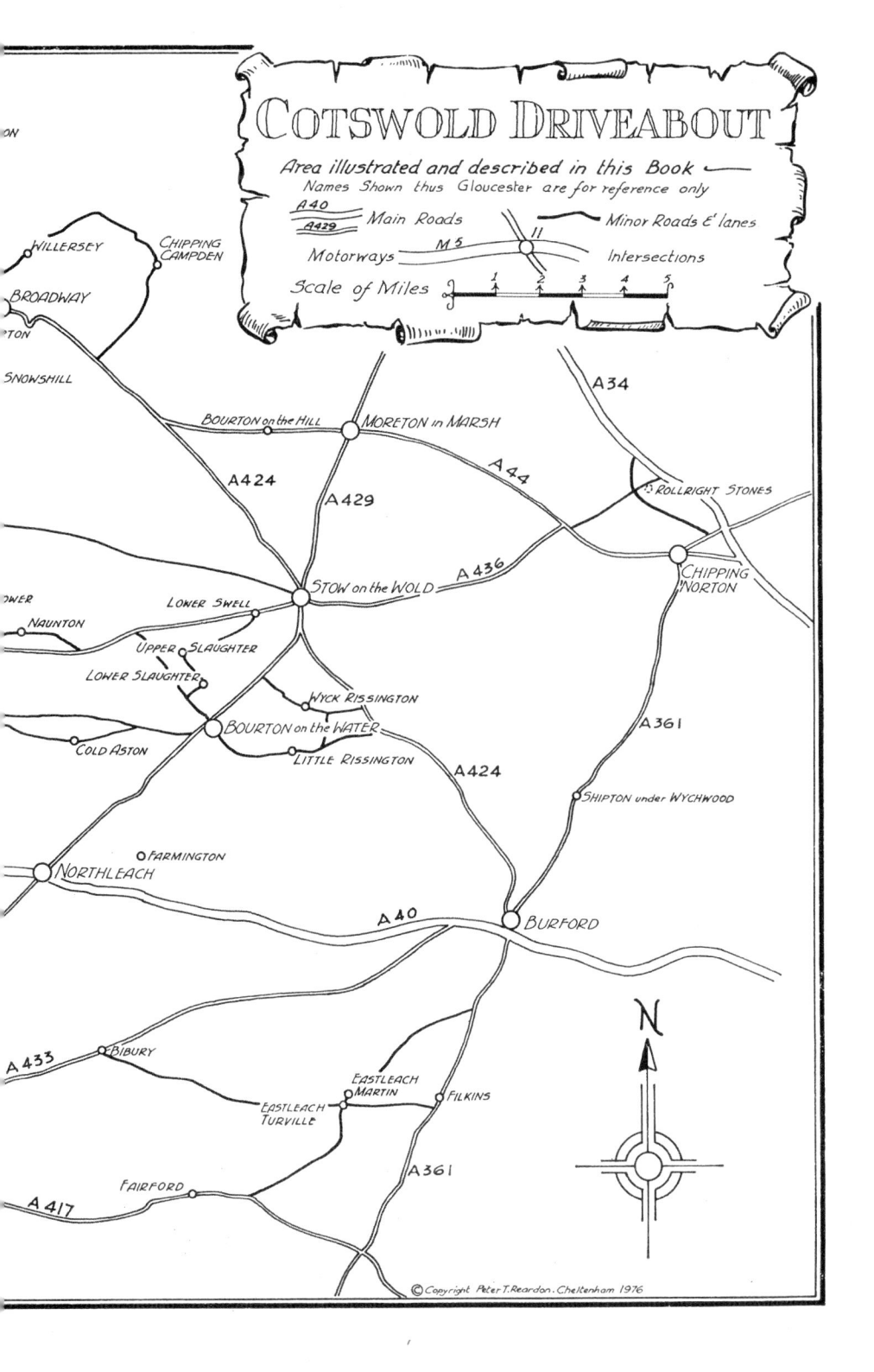

Area illustrated and described in this Book
Names Shown thus Gloucester are for reference only

A40 / A429 — Main Roads
Motorways — M5
Minor Roads & lanes
Intersections

Scale of Miles 0 1 2 3 4 5

© Copyright Peter T. Reardon, Cheltenham 1976

Gloucester Cathedral from the South West

Gloucester

Gloucester, the county town, has a history going back to before Roman times. When they came they made Glevum, as it was known then, into a military stronghold. The Saxons came and in the 7th century established a monastry which the Normans restyled in the late 11th century, when the Cathedral was built. This is almost all that remains of the once great Abbey of St. Peter, due to the Dissolution in Henry VIII's time. The main picture shows the Cathedral flanked by the warehouses in Gloucester Docks. Ships up to 1000 tons can still be accepted in this, the most inland port in the country, via the august Gloucester and Sharpness Canal.

KING EDWARD'S TOWER

The small sketch shows the 13th century King Edward's Tower by the Cathedral. This City is well worth a visit from anyone coming to the Cotswolds, as there are attractions to suit everyone, from an up-to-date Shopping Centre to the National Waterways Museum, just one of the many attractions in the revitalised Victorian Docklands of Gloucester.

Hailes Abbey

The little drawing on the right does not really portray the grandeur associated with the ruins of something like an Abbey. It does however, show the excellent state of preservation of some of the details to be found. The section shown is part of the drainage system of the old Abbey, having continuously running water. This was probably supplied from a spring starting near Little Farmcote on the hills above, the water course being diverted to the Abbey then flowing on to the River Isbourne which joins the Avon at Evesham in Worcestershire. Hailes Abbey lies about a mile off to the right of the A46, 2 miles north of Winchcombe on the road to Broadway. The Abbey is National Trust property though cared for by English Heritage.

Lechlade

The little bridge pictured here on the right carries the A361 Burford to Swindon road over the River Thames at Lechlade. Built in 1792, it was at one time a toll bridge, when a halfpenny had to be paid before a traveller was allowed to cross to the other side. The toll keeper lived in the house attached to the bridge as shown in the drawing, and the upkeep of the bridge and house was paid for by the tolls collected from the wayfarers. This bridge lies south of Lechlade and about half a mile from where the old Severn and Thames canal joined the Rivers Thames and Coln. At this junction one of the old Round Houses, built for the lengthsmen on the canal, still exists in good condition and is occupied.

Leckhampton Hill

Part of the Cotswolds, with the escarpment facing north and west, Leckhampton Hill is very popular with not only the visitors to Cheltenham and the area, but also with the local people. It has featured in several roles, that of fortified camp during the Iron Age, a place of work, there being a quarry worked here for about 130 years, as a battleground, when there were fights and violent protests over public rights of way and finally, as a pleasure ground for people to enjoy the views, air and sheer gratification of walking across the top of the 965ft. hill. On the west facing escarpment is the Devil's Chimney, a massive rock formation making a popular landmark. Much evidence remains of the days when quarrying was a thriving industry on the hill, the old lime kilns pictured here from above being perhaps one of the most prominent man made relics surviving today. Many fine buildings standing in Cheltenham today have been constructed of this local stone. The quarry was operative for about 130 years, giving employment to local men and bringing much business to Cheltenham finally closed in 1928.

The Long Stone

Woodchester, Avening, Bisley are names of places near Stroud where antiquities seem to abound. They are there for all to see, each having its own story to tell, but they must be looked for and all but the casual observer should be able to find them. Such a one is illustrated on the right and is known as the Long Stone. The legend surrounding this stone is that it had strange healing powers, especially where the disease of rickets is concerned. In medieval times, a newborn child would be passed through the hole in the stone, as it was believed that by doing so the child would be protected from the malady for the rest of it's life. The stone is large, about 8 ft. high, and stands in one corner of a field just off the road. If the road is taken from Minchinhampton to Avening, the Long Stone can be found in the field on the left hand side just before the hamlet of Hampton Fields.

Minchinhampton

Minchinhampton is probably best known for the common (N.T.), nearly 600 acres of land. The small drawing is of Tom Long's Post at the junction of six roads on the common, in memory of Tom Long, highwayman, who took his own life at that spot rather than be captured. Also one can see Iron Age earthworks called the Bulwarks and an Iron Age Camp fort at Amberley. A Long Barrow, damaged, is at the north end. There is a golf course and plenty of room for family fun and games or just for walks. The town has many fine buildings which owe their existence to the great days of wool in the 17th century.

The Market House, built in 1698 is still used today. The Church of the Holy Trinity is worth a look while in town, and over the page our main picture is of the Cross in the Market Square, Minchinhampton.

— The MARKET SQUARE, MINCHINHAMPTON —

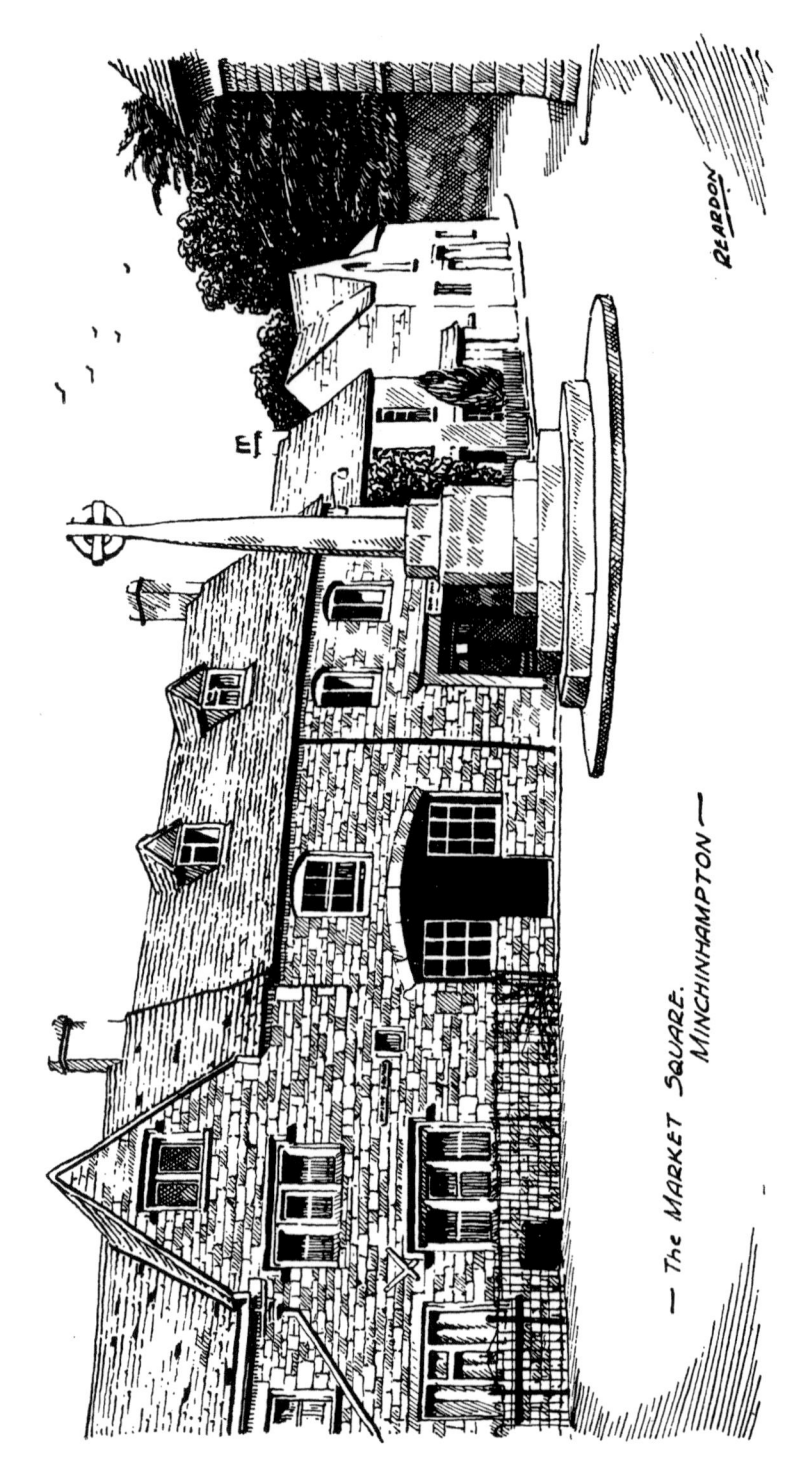

Northleach

Shown here on the right is perhaps an odd-angle view of the picturesque old world Sherborne Arms set overlooking the Square in Northleach. Made wealthy and famous by the wool merchants of the middle ages, the town has changed little, and there is no doubt this little house of refreshment has witnessed many a good and bad deal, both on the market square and within it's walls. Although now renovated and taking in the adjoining forge as a restaurant, none of the charm has been lost in so doing. While in Northleach, a look at a house of a different kind would be interesting — a house of detention.

Built 400 years ago it is unfortunately now just a relic of the past. Not very comfortable but larger than some that are still about, the dweller never stayed long. Usually a day and a night was the term and this was decided by the Northleach Court Leet, which was the local government of the day. The Northleach Court Leet is still active today. The Lord of the Leet is Earl Bathurst, whose family has held this position as far back as the Dissolution of the Monastries. Today, the High Steward summons 12 men to meet on a specified day in November, to hold court as has been done through the centuries. There is a written constitution of 39 laws which can still be enforced since they have never been repealed by any government up to now. It was these laws, and probably others besides, that put people in this little place — The Old Lockup — to be found in a corner of the Market Place, right by the Post Office. In those days there was a market cross where the War Memorial now stands in the opposite corner of the square to the Sherborne Arms. The Northleach Court Leet has records going back to the 16th century, with entries like 'John Proffyt was fined 6/8d. because wife tooks lbs of butter 'ere the Market Cross', and 1638, a record of 6 pence being paid for faggott to burn deceased pig.

Painswick

All through history there has been a trail of people who have done wrong in some way or another. The punishment meted out was dependant on the severity of the crime. Sometimes prison was too severe for petty crimes and a cooling of fervour was all that was needed. 24 hours in the stocks was of course the ideal answer. The stocks shown in the sketch are called spectacle stocks because of their similarity in appearance to a pair of spectacles. This sample, possibly the only one in existence in this country, can be seen behind the wall on the north east corner of the Parish churchyard at Painswick. Famous also for the hundred fine yews in the churchyard there is also an interesting lych gate. Painswick is a delightful Cotswold town nestling on the A46 Cheltenham to Stroud road.

Prinknash Abbey

About 7 miles south of Cheltenham on the A46 lies Prinknash Park, owned by a community of Benedictine monks. In the grounds stands the new Prinknash Abbey, massive in its simplicity and dignity. There is an excellent pottery and gift shop open to the public where Prinknash made pottery in great variety can be bought. Adjoining the shop is the tea room where a cup of tea or a lunch can be had at the appropriate time. Behind the tea room and shop on a lower floor level is the works offering pleasant working conditions with up to date equipment. Here the monks produce ware for sale not only in the shop but for export to many countries in the world. The bells shown right have been moved to a new site by the Abbey after over 45 years at the original Prinknash Abbey.

The Rollright Stones

This single stone shown here in this sketch stands nearly 9ft. high and is just over 5ft. wide. It is known as the King Stone and takes its place with two companion groups known as the Circle with seventy-odd stones, and the Whispering Knights, a group of five some quarter of a mile away. These are collectively known as the famous Rollright Stones. The legend surrounding the stones is that a witch met a King and his army whose intention it was to rule all England. The witch, not being in favour of this, made a bargain with him, that he take seven long strides and 'if Long Compton thou cans't see, King of England thou shalt be'. Long Compton couldn't be seen from the seventh stride so the King, his men and the Whispering Knights were all turned to stone. So goes the legend, but in fact it is more likely to be as the little plaque describes in the front of the circle, a Bronze Age stone circle for ritual purposes dating back to about 1500 BC. It is for sure very old, and some amusement can be had trying to count the number of stones in the circle, as it is claimed that the same number can never be counted twice. All the stones are now a National Monument and are in the care of the Department of the Environment. There is plenty of parking right alongside for visitors. The stones are to be found just north of Chipping Norton by about three miles and to the west of the A34. Contrary to much general thinking, the Rollright Stones are not in Gloucestershire, though they are as much a part of the Cotswolds as Chipping Campden, Cirencester and Stow-on-the-Wold. The Circle and the Whispering Knights are in Oxfordshire while just across the road the King Stone stands in Warwickshire. The little drawing on the right depicts a few of the stones in the circle looking west to east. Long Compton lies about a mile to the north of the Rollright Stones.

Severn and Thames Canal

This canal was a project designed to enable conveyance of bulk goods from Bristol to London without making a coastal trip by sea. The canal ran from Framilode on the Severn to Lechlade on the Thames, a distance of 26 miles, and involved the construction of a tunnel from Sapperton, under Hailey Wood to Coates, 2¼ miles away. Built around 1785, it was later bought by the G.W.R. and closed in 1893. In 1911 the last boat went through the tunnel and the canal became derelict. The picture shows the Sapperton end of the tunnel, about 5 miles west of Cirencester just off the A419. For the boating enthusiast there has been a lot of discussion and to date some work has been carried out in an attempt to re-open the canal and tunnel for leisure sailing.

Southam Leper Chute

The drawing below shows a leper chute, a protruding little structure not often seen in these times. This one can be seen on the wall of a fine tythe barn at Southam just north of Cheltenham off the A46 Winchcombe road. The reason for using a chute of this kind was that lepers could be given their ration of food without having to come into contact with their benefactor. The barn was used by monks for keeping sotres, and this gives rise to the thought that at one time there may have been a monastery or been a monastery or similar abbey at Southam.

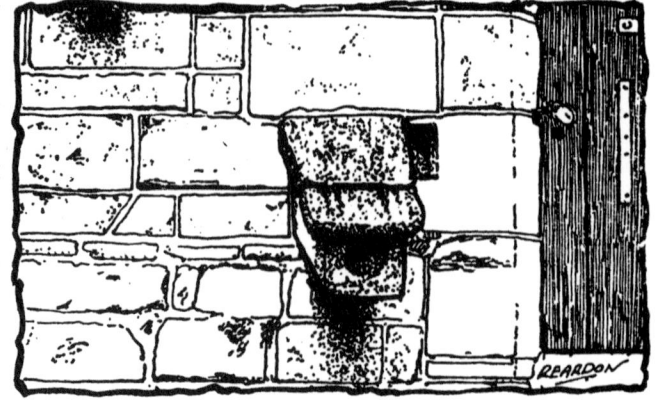

Stow on the Wold

Stow on the Wold "where the wind blows cold", and at 800 feet above sea level this local saying can at times be very true, but cold or not, this town is a must for any visitor to the area. It has all the charms a Cotswold Town should have, from Town Square where the old town stocks stand, to Cotswold Church full of Civil War history. Stow figured in the 1642-1649 Civil War by St. Edward's Church being used for the prison of Sir Jacob Astley and about 1200 of his men in 1646. The little sketch depicts the North door of St. Edward's Church. A look at the town will show you a Lantern headed Market Cross which has been standing in the Square since about the 14th century. It was restored a hundred years ago in memory of Sir Joseph Chamberlain, who donated to the provision of an up-to-date water supply.

Tewkesbury

Tewkesbury is a wonderful little town with its history going back to Norman times when the great Abbey of St. Mary the Virgin was built. The tower, the finest and largest Norman tower in the country, stands nearly 150 feet high. A look round this town will reveal many interesting buildings, some that have figured in either true history or novels. On the east side of the A38, opposite Gupshill Manor, is the site of Margarets Camp, and at the end of Lower Lode Lane, on the left, is the Bloody Meadow - both relics of the wars of the Roses 1445-85. Pictured overleaf is the Church of St. Mary the Virgin looking S-E. The little picture shows a footbridge across the River Swilgate near Priors Park. Tewkesbury today is a busy and expanding town, with a big pleasure boating business and industry at nearby Newtown and Northway.

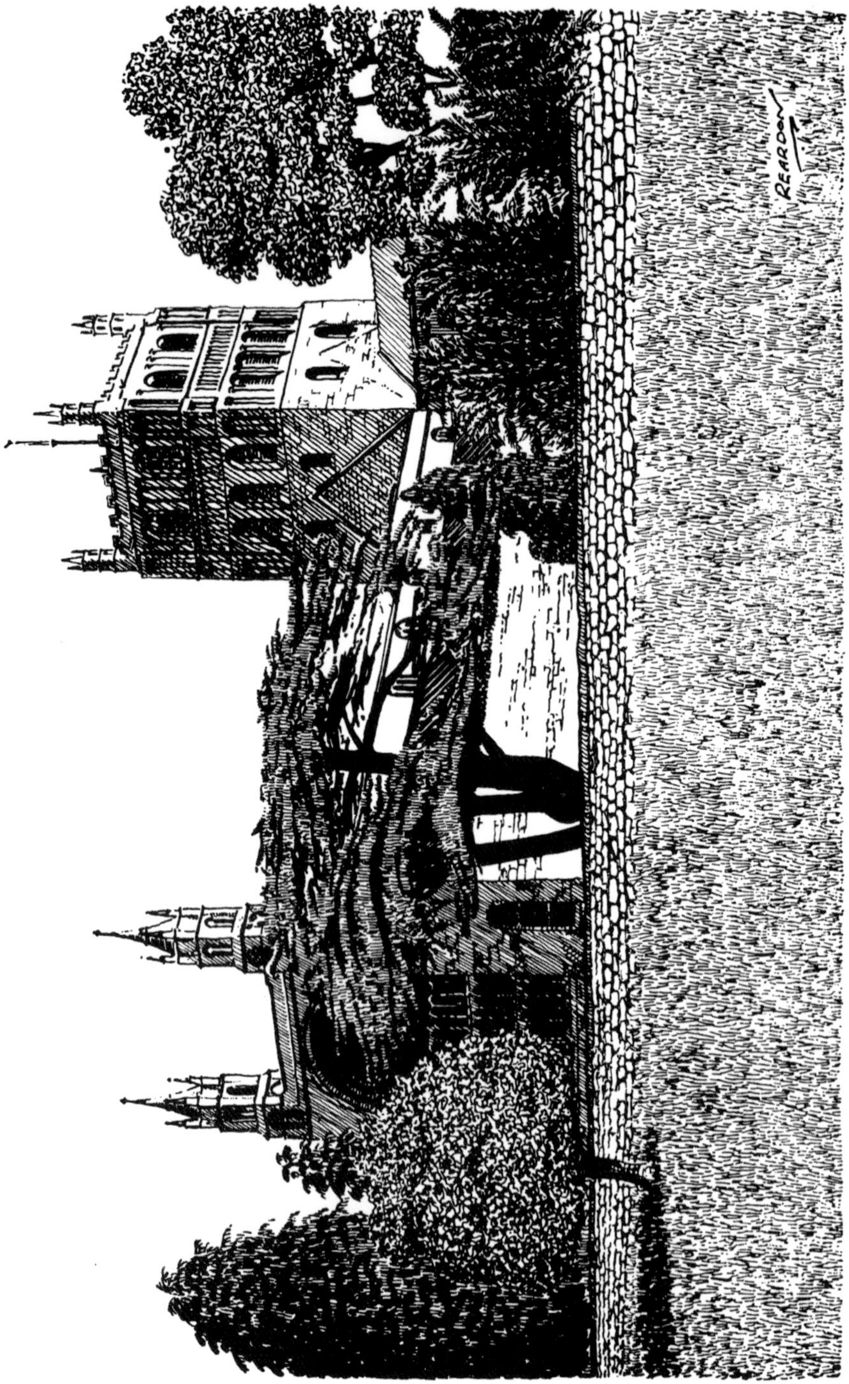
REARDON

Winchcombe

The little drawing on the right depicts the town clock in Winchcombe and may be seen in the High Street, on the front wall of the Town Hall, just a few steps from Vineyard Street, and on the junction with North Street, the B4078. The clock was presented to the town by a very wealthy stockbroker, Mr. Reginald Prance, about 100 years ago. Mr. Prance, who lived at nearby Stanley Pontlarge, was an extremely benevolent citizen, at one time giving £70,000 to Tewkesbury Abbey among other notable public-spirited deeds. The old stocks pictured in the little sketch bottom right may be seen in a small railed enclosure right at the road junction adjoining the Town Hall. Almost opposite is the George, once a pilgrim inn in the days of Hailes Abbey close by, now in ruins.

Winchcombe has a setting which obviously inspired people all through the ages to want to settle here. Two Roman villas to the south, an abbey at Hailes to the north-east, Sudeley Castle to the south-east, a hill fort about 3 miles to the south at Roel and a Stone Age burial chamber called Belas Knap on Cleeve Hill to the south. The ruins of Hailes Abbey is now in National Trust care and managed by English Heritage. Winchcombe spans the A46 some 7 miles north of Cheltenham. The main picture over the page shows Vineyard Street, the approach to Sudeley.

Sudeley Castle provides a wonderful day out with many exciting events taking place during the summer. The castle was once the home of Katherine Parr, the last wife of Henry VIII. Elizabeth I as a child lived at Sudeley and also the unfortunate Lady Jane Grey who accompanied Katherine Parr to Sudeley in the hope that she would marry Edward VI. Sudeley Castle is one of the major attractions of the Cotswolds and is well worth a visit.

'THE ROAD TO SUDELEY',
VINEYARD STREET, WINCHCOMBE, GLOS.

INDEX

	Page		Page
Bibury	5	Lechlade	20
Bisley	5	Leckhampton Hill	20
Bourton on the Water	7	Long Stone	21
Broadway Tower	8	Lower Slaughter	6, 7
Burford	8		
		Map	16, 17
		Minchinhampton	21, 22
Cainscross	9	Moreton in Marsh	15
Chipping Campden	9		
Cheltenham Spa	10, 11, 20	Northleach	23
Cirencester	12		
Compton Abdale	13	Painswick	24
Country Code	32	Prinknash Abbey	24
Didbrook	13	Rollright Stones	25
		Roman Road	12
Filkins	14, 15		
Four Shires Stone	15	Severn and Thames Canal	26
		Southam	26
Gloucester	18, 19	Spectacle Stocks	24
		Stow on the Wold	27
		Tewkesbury	27, 28
Hailes Abbey	19	Tom Long's Post	21
Index	31	Winchcombe	29, 30

Writer, Artist and Publisher
Peter Reardon

Peter Reardon is not just a Cotswold Artist but is the co-founder of Reardon publishing the Cotswold publishers and has had his work travel to the four corners of the world.

The Company's very first book published in 1976 was a predecessor to this publication Cotswold Driveabout.